Rumi

HIDDEN MUSIC

Rumi

HIDDEN MUSIC

Translated by

Azima Melita Kolin

& Maryam Mafi

Thorsons

Thorsons
An Imprint of HarperCollins*Publishers*
77-85 Fulham Palace Road,
Hammersmith, London W6 8JB

The Thorsons website address is: www.thorsons.com

First published 2001

1 3 5 7 9 10 8 6 4 2

Text copyright © Azima Melita Kolin and Maryam Mafi, 2001
Copyright © HarperCollins Publishers Ltd 2001

Azima Melita Kolin and Maryam Mafi assert the moral right to
be identified as the authors of this work

A catalogue record of this book
is available from the British Library
ISBN 0 00 712032 X

Printed and bound in Hong Kong

Calligraphy by Hassan Behrast Shayjani
Emblem Artwork by Nuran Gungorençan
Book Cover and Paintings by Azima Melita Kolin

Contents

Acknowledgements

We would like to thank all the lovers of Rumi without whom this book would not have come into fruition. The participants in the readings who gave much of their time, love and help in forming and editing the programmes: Ann Marie Terry, Latifa Wirgman, Gina Landor, Stewart Pearce, Uta Schlichtig and Sabiha Rumani Malik. Hernan Andreu, Lola Ceva, Dorian Keller, Alia Beger, Werner Freundt and Regina Hornbereger for their translations into Spanish and German. Special thanks to Aziz for his continuous support and love. Our deepest thanks to M. Bordbar who generously offered his time and wisdom in clarifying the Farsi text and his wife, Forouzandeh for making it possible; LMSR Nezam Mafi, for their constant encouragement and love. We would like to thank Hugh, Elena and Vincent Macleod, Alexandre, Mahsima and Jean-Marc Fraysse for their love and tolerance.

Our thanks to our editor, Carole Tonkinson, for her enthusiasm and trust. And finally, our gratitude to all Rumi lovers who attended our concerts and inspired us to continue with our translations.

We would like to dedicate the chapter "Someone is Hidden Inside" to the memory of Reza Gholi.

Introduction

What did Rumi have to say that appeals to us today, 700 years later? His words trouble, pierce, console and uplift the heart. He speaks of a love that can only be attained if it is lived beyond all the limitations of intellect and beyond any divisions of dogma.

Rumi is the teacher of love, the love that he finds *difficult to convey the magic of to those who are made of dust.* Yet he takes the dust and moulds it into *white silent lilies that speak the truth.* The power and beauty of his words come from experience; he knows the wounds of life and has gone beyond them to find the ecstasy of love. According to Rumi, love is the most difficult concept to define. "My pen splinters when I write Love." Yet from this love, Rumi's poems burst like stars and fill the sky like the bright and clear stars in the desert night. Each poem takes us into a different world and always in love. Like Rumi who found in Shams his only Friend, his water of life and the music of his soul, we too find in Rumi the friend who quenches the thirst of our soul and we fall in love.

Born Jalaludin Mohamad on 30th September 1207 in Balkh a city in the Persian Empire, he was brought up a Sufi by his father and became a brilliant and respected jurist. Rumi was 37 when he met a highly advanced spiritual master in the form of the dervish, Shams. Shams was the soul mate, the inspiration that Rumi had been waiting for. He was an enigmatic figure in his sixties, a wandering mystic walking on the path of love. His appearance was shabby and his manner rough and uncompromising. He had searched the world for someone who could receive his wisdom and become his spiritual confidant. He found that person in Rumi and Rumi found in Shams the embodiment of God's beauty, in him he saw the face of God. Shams opened new dimensions of divine love to Rumi and showed him the direct path to the Beloved through the heart. He showed him an ecstatic way of worship through poetry, music, Sama or meditative whirling and freed him from the restraints of piety and self-renunciation. No one will ever know what passed between them but the poetry in the Divan and Masnavi that flowed from Rumi are the only true testimony of the love they shared for the Divine.

Shams' disappearance and subsequent death was the catalyst for Rumi's extraordinary outpour of longing and love that eventually led him to the ultimate union with the Beloved. To achieve ultimate union with the Beloved, the Lover must surrender all sense of self and become the Beloved.

"You are my face, small wonder that I cannot see you..."

For many years we have been presenting concerts based on Farsi and English reading of Rumi's poems. These concerts have been a way of bringing Rumi's teaching to the public. Our first book of translations *Whispers of the Beloved* and now, *Hidden Music*, arise from the same urge to share the beauty of Rumi's message of Love as the One divine unifying force. We hope that you will hear the hidden music on this journey.

Azima Melita Kolin and Maryam Mafi

Sun

and

Moon

Shams has come!
My Sun and Moon, my sight and hearing
that Beauty suddenly appeared by my side.
The one who was always in my thoughts
for whom I've searched so long
has come to me with open arms
laying flowers on my path.
My deepest wish has been granted.
What can I fear when my shield
my water of life has come?
Today is a day of Glory!
Today I am like Solomon
with the ring of abundance on my finger
and the divine crown on my head.
I can fly for he has given me wings
I can roar like a lion, I can rise like dawn.
No more verses
for I am taken to a place from where
this world seems so small…

My heart is like a lute
each chord crying with longing and pain.
My Beloved is watching me
wrapped in silence.

Come, come
the Beloved has arrived!
The rose garden is blooming
run and offer your life and the world
to the rising Sun.
Smile and see the beauty hidden
in an ugly face,
weep, weep for those who have turned
away from love.
What a day, what a day!
A day of resurrection!
The lover has once again broken free from his chains.
The scroll of our deeds brought by the angels lays open.
Beat the drum and say no more
the heart and mind have gone
the soul has flown to the Beloved!

One day I feel confused and down,
the next I can reach the sky
without you I am never calm.
In your absence people ridicule me,
but when you come
I don't mind what they think or say.
I refuse to feast or be merry without my Beloved.
However he appears I will follow.
If he comes as a cupbearer, I'll become one too
if he comes as an ascetic, I'll become a pious pilgrim.
If he pretends to be a madman, I'll become a perfect fool
if he tries to escape, I will become a mighty hunter.
Yet, when I complain about my sleepless nights
he mocks me and says I do not pray enough,
when I ask him for a favor he sends me off.
What am I to do but to surrender
to the will of my Beloved.

If this me is not I, then
who am I?
If I am not the one who speaks, then
who does?
If this me is only a robe then
who is
the one I am covering?

Come my Master, come don't turn away from me,
come my deceitful Moon!
Look at this forlorn and thirsty lover,
come my drunken King!
You are my life, my senses, you are everything!
Be the rising Moon in my dark nights
I am thirsty for your light.
Use my hands, look through my eyes,
listen with my ears.
You are the soul of every living thing.
Come, come back dancing like the rays of the Sun
and chase away the shadows.
You are the banner of the New World
and the mind is at your feet.
Come back my love
my broken heart cannot bear more passion,
no more promises.

I've had enough of sleepless nights,
of my unspoken grief, of my tired wisdom.
Come my treasure, my breath of life
come and dress my wounds and be my cure.
Enough of words.
Come to me without a sound.

Last night
my Beloved was like the Moon
so beautiful!
He was even brighter than the Sun.
His grace is far beyond my grasp
the rest is silence.

I smile like a flower not only with my lips
but with my whole being
for I am alone with the King and
have lost myself in him.

At dawn your flame seized my heart
but left behind my body.
I will shout and raise havoc until
you come back for me tonight.

My Beloved, do not let anger estrange my heart
be generous, invite me to your feast.
Let no one be deprived of the joy
of your company.

If the face of the Beloved
does not make you gasp in wonder
and laugh ecstatically with joy
then you must be like a stone
good only for building prison walls.

When you show your face
even the stones begin to dance with joy.
When you lift your veil
the wise ones lose themselves in awe.
The reflection of your face turns the water
into a golden shimmer
and softens even the fire into a tender glow.
When I see your face,
the Moon and the few floating stars around it
lose their glory.
The Moon is far too old and dim
to be compared with a mirror.
Your breath touched my soul and
I saw beyond all limits.
In your presence Mars,
the god of war sits peacefully
by the side of Venus.

I am a sculptor
I carve new shapes and forms each day
but when I see you they all melt.

I am a painter
I create images and bring them to life
but when I see you they all vanish.

Who are you my Friend
the promised lover or the deceitful enemy?
You ruin everything I build.
My soul has sprung from yours and
it carries the scent of your perfume.
But without you my heart is shattered,
please, come back or let me leave
this lonely world.

I am hopelessly in love with you, no point
giving me advice.
I have drunk love's poison, no point
taking any remedy.
They want to chain my feet but
what's the point
when it is my heart that's gone mad!

Love means to reach for the sky and
with every breath to tear a hundred veils.
Love means to step away from the ego,
to open the eyes of inner vision and
not to take this world so seriously.

Congratulations dear heart!
You have joined the circle of lovers,
tell me in your own words
when did all this throbbing begin?

"I was absorbed in my work in this world
but I never lost my longing for home.
One day, exhausted with no strength left,
I was lifted suddenly by the grace of Love.
To describe this mystery there are no words."

With every word, you break my heart.
You see my story
written in blood on my face,
why do you ignore it,
do you have a heart of stone?

I am the slave of that perfect Moon!
Don't talk to me of suffering, I don't want to hear.
Talk about light, joy and sweetness
and if you can't, keep silent!

Last night Love found me shouting, mad
and beyond myself, and said:
"I am here, why are you so worried and afraid?"
O Love, I am overwhelmed with fear.
"Be silent, let me whisper a secret in your ear,
just nod your head and don't say a word."

Oh how delicate, how subtle is the path of love!
This most precious Moon-like beauty appeared to me!

My heart, is this the Moon or my imagination?
"Be silent, it is not for you to understand
don't you see, you have been blessed."
But what is this, the face of an angel or a man?

"Be silent, what you see is beyond angels or men."
But what is it, tell me, or I will go out of my mind.
"Do not torment yourself, leave this house of illusions
and say no more."
"O please", I begged, "tell me, is this the face of God?"
My heart nodded silently.

Free my heart from the entanglement
of search and disappointment.
Bring me the wine of love
and my soul will open its wings.
You have the perfect cup for every lover.

I was seeking knowledge
when that beautiful one appeared.
I tried to charm him and asked:
Would you kindly interpret the dream
I had last night, you are my only confidant.

He shook his head and smiled
as if he could see through me and said:
'Don't try to charm me,
I see every nuance, every color and scent.
I am your mirror.'

In his hands I become the design he weaves
with golden thread,
I become his living masterpiece.

Sometimes I call you my cup, sometimes
the jug, sometimes my precious gold,
sometimes my silver moon.
Sometimes I call you a seed, sometimes
the prey and sometimes a trap.
And all this is because
I don't want to call you by your name.

Bring back to me my fleeting lover
make up excuses, sing him beautiful songs,
convince this exquisite Moon
to come back home.

Do not be deceived by his charming promises
he can easily bewitch water
and tie air into a knot.
But when you see his Sun-like face
watch how God's wonders appear!

My heart, go gently and when you find
my priceless treasure
offer him my absolute devotion.

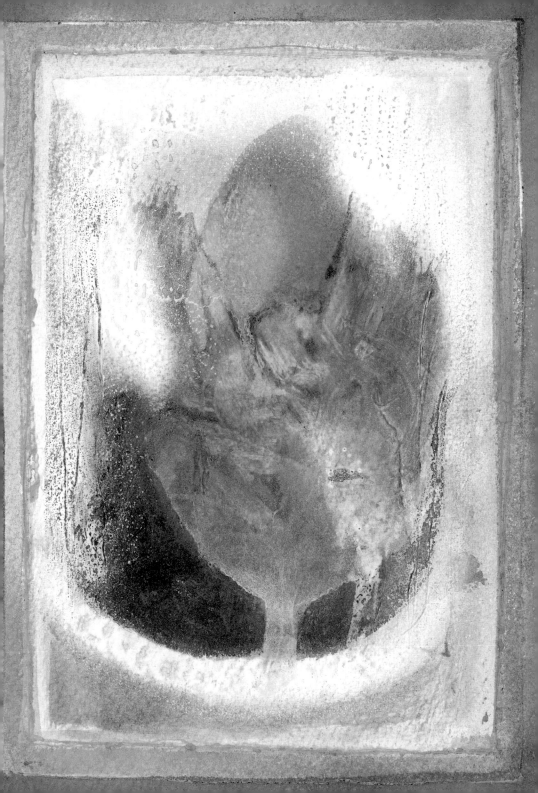

Go to sleep,
let me be alone with my Beloved.
Leave this spent old man, tossed
by the waves of love all night.
Be cruel or forgive me, but keep away
do not, like me, fall into the trap of love
choose the safe road of life.
Leave me with my tears
in the lonely corner of love's sorrow,
my choice has been made.
The Beloved can be harsh but
He is the Ultimate Lover
never expect Him to be faithful.
But you, worn out lover, be patient and endure
there is no help or cure for this pain
other than dying to yourself.

In a dream last night I saw the Master.
He called me to come closer and said:
"Love is an emerald.
Its brilliant light wards off dragons
on this treacherous path,
only for those who are truly in love."
But my worthy scholar, if you are tired of listening,
keep telling your own stories instead.

He is back
the One who was never absent,
the water that never left the stream,
the essence of the musk
of which we are the scent.
Can the essence and the scent
be separate?

The Path

Open the door, a novice has arrived!
Offer me a cup of wine and walk with me
for a while.
You don't mind long distances because
on the way you lay your traps,
and plan how to break my heart.
You fulfilled hundreds of my wishes, yet my heart
still hungers for more.
Your kindness warms and blesses everyone
even the sun bows before you.
Please, let me be your slave and silently walk
by your side.
I will find new meaning in every joy and sorrow.
In that silence
I will hear the voice of spirit, and freed
from this world
I will see another order where the end is
another beginning.

The early breeze before dawn
is the keeper of secrets.
Don't go back to sleep!
It is time for prayer, it is time to ask for
what you really need.
Don't go back to sleep!
The door of the One who created the world
is always open.
Don't go back to sleep.

O Friend, You made me lovingly
You clothed me in a robe of skin and blood
then planted deep inside me
a seed from Your heart.
You turned the whole world
into a sanctuary where
You are the only One.

My love, you are closer to me than myself,
you shine through my eyes.
Your light is brighter than the Moon.
Step into the garden
so all the flowers, even the tall poplar
can kneel before your beauty.
Let your voice silence the lily
famous for its hundred tongues.
When you want to be kind you are
softer than the soul but when you withdraw
you can be so cold and harsh.

Dear one, you can be wild and rebellious but
when you meet him face to face
his charm will make you docile like the earth.
Throw away your shield and bare your chest
there is no stronger protection than him.

That's why when the dervish withdraws
from the world he covers all the cracks in the wall,
so the outside light cannot come through.
He knows that only the inner light
illuminates his world.

I asked for a kiss,
you gave me six.
Whose pupil were you
to become such a master?
Full of kindness, generosity…
You are not of this world.

به نام آنکه جان را فکرت آموخت

چراغ دل به نور جان برافروخت

ز فضلش هر دو عالم گشت روشن

ز فیضش خاک آدم گشت گلشن

توانایی که در یک طرفةالعین

ز کاف و نون پدید آورد کونین

Deafened by the voice of desire
you are unaware the Beloved lives
in the core of your heart.
Stop the noise and
you will hear His voice
in the silence.

All friends have vanished.
Like fleeting thoughts they scattered
and left me only with the thought
of my Beloved.
Now alone with every breath
I call the only Friend of the forsaken.
I was taken by the stream of love
I tasted the fruit of love's tree,
surrounded with such tenderness, such sweetness
I even had to chase the wasps away!
I was the doorkeeper at the gate of my Beloved.
He left, and now bewildered
I don't know which way to turn.

There is no wine without You,
no use for the rosary without Your hand.
From afar You order me to dance
but unless You set the stage and
open the curtain, my Beloved,
how can I dance?

You are the light of my heart
and the comfort of my soul,
but you are such a troublemaker.
Why ask me, "Have you seen the Friend?"
When you know so well that
the Friend can not be seen.

Those of you who feel no love
sleep on.
Those of you who do not feel the sorrow of love
in whose heart passion has never risen
sleep on.
Those who do not long for union
who are not constantly asking, 'Where is He?'
sleep on.
Love's path is outside of all religious sects
if trickery and hypocrisy is your way
sleep on.
If you don't melt like copper in your quest
for the alchemical gold
sleep on.
If like a drunkard you fall left and right
unaware the night has passed and it's time for prayer
sleep on.
Fate has taken my sleep but since
it has not taken yours, young man
sleep on.

We have fallen into love's hands
since you are in your own
sleep on.
I am the one who is drunk on Love
since you are drunk on food
sleep on.
I have given up my head and have nothing more to say
but you can wrap yourself in the robe of words and
sleep on.

Invoking Your name
does not help me to see You.
I'm blinded by the light of Your face.
Longing for Your lips
does not bring them any closer.
What veils You from me
is my vision of You.

The guest of honor is no more
my cup is empty
no more intimacy of soul to soul.
His piercing look, his elegance and splendor,
his kindness and exquisite words
captured my heart.
Where is your love, he asked me,
what holds you back, where is your glory?
Why are you still absorbed by earthly concerns
when the hour of truth has arrived?

I drown in the sea of his generosity
clothes are a burden when swimming,
how heavy are my robe and turban!
It is the essence of the rose
that pulls me to the rose garden.
Only Love gives value to wealth and power.

My wise Master, you are a Lion,
you are my King, I am your humble servant
you can destroy me, you can create me anew.
My heart do not complain,
don't speak of this and that, go beyond
the impressions, look only
for the essence.

Dear heart, you are so unreasonable!
First you fall in love then worry about your life.
You rob and steal then worry about the law.
You profess to be in love
yet still worry about what people say.

From all that was familiar,
I broke away
Now I am lost, without a place,
wandering.
With no music like a fool I dance
and clap my hands.
How am I to live without You?
You are everywhere but
I cannot see You.

O lovers
Love will lay a carpet of treasures under your feet.
Musicians
Love will fill your drums with gold.
Thirsty ones
Love will turn your scorched desert
into a meadow of paradise.
Forsaken ones
Love will open the doors to the King's palace.
Alchemists
Love's alchemy will reshape gallows into altars.
Sinners
Love will change your apathy to faith.
Kings of the world
in love's hands you will melt like a candle.

To the parched lips of those who are
willing to surrender
Love will bring the wine that changes darkness
into vision, cruelty into compassion
and dust into precious incense.

Those who think the heart is only in the chest
take two or three steps and are content.
The rosary, the prayer rug and repentance
are paths that they mistake for the destination.

Walking in the garden with my lover
I was distracted by a rose.
My love scolded me saying,
"How could you look at a rose
with my face so close?"

I am love's musician playing for joy
I comb the beard of happiness
and pull the moustache of sorrow.
When my core is touched by music
love's wine begins to flow.
In this temple of fire my blood
is melting the snow from my body.
It is spring, it is time for action,
it is time to throw away all false pretences.
Dragged and pulled in love, I bear all the pain.
Caught in this confusion, in this bitter sweetness
I am the captive of this journey.
It is the scent of home that keeps me going
the hope of union, the face of my Beloved.
I know our fate is separation, but until my last breath
I will search for my sweet love,
I will seek my home.

With love you cannot bargain
there, the choice is not yours.
Love is a mirror, it reflects
only your essence,
if you have the courage
to look in its face.

I will run fast and will keep running until
I catch up with the riders.
I will dissolve into air and become nothing
so I can reach my Beloved.
I will become fire, burn my house
and head for the desert.
I will become all pain, so I can be healed.
I will become humble and turn into soil
so your flowers can grow in me.
I will kiss the ground and become water
so I can flow to your rose garden.
I will make my face shine like a gold coin
so I can become worthy of my Beloved.
I came in this world helpless and fearful
but at the end of this journey I will find safety.
The blessing of truth is like water
it flows downstream.
I came to this earth so that I can find the way back
to my Beloved.

Whisper to me intimately, like a lover
for tenderness is rare in this world.
It is difficult to convey the magic of love
to those who are made of dust.

Plant

the Seed

of Truth

If you never searched for truth
come with us
and you will become a seeker.
If you were never a musician
come with us
and you will find your voice.
You may posses immense wealth
come with us
and you will become love's beggar.
You may think yourself a master
come with us
and love will turn you into a slave.
If you've lost your spirit,
come with us
take off your silk coverings,
put on our rough cloak
and we will bring you back to life.

In our gathering one candle lights hundreds,
we will light your path and give you courage
so you will open like a flower
and join in our joyous laughter.
Plant the seed of truth and watch it grow
when it spreads its branches
come with us and sit under the blossoms.
Your eyes will open to the secret of Truth.

The Friend who cannot be seen is the most
subtle and precious.
The work that cannot be seen is the most
refined.
The cleverest of all is the one who does not
deceive himself
for he has deceived deceit.

My soul is a mirror that reveals secrets,
I may not speak about them but
cannot deny knowing.
I run away from body and soul
where I belong, I swear, I do not know.
Seeker, if you want to know the *secret*,
first you must die to your self.
You may see me but do not think I am here
I have vanished into my Beloved
graced by the essence of love.
My arched back is the bow and my words,
the unbending arrows aimed at Truth.
My tears are testimony of my devotion to Shams
and from those tears white lilies will grow
that will speak the Truth.

Seek the wisdom
that will untie your knot
seek the path
that demands your whole being.
Leave that which is not, but appears
to be
seek that which is, but is
not apparent.

I will give up anything to win your love
but if you say no,
I will accept and walk away filled with
the sweetness of your denial.
I have come secretly to seize your flame for my soul
I have come to steal from the King's treasure
but if I do not succeed,
I will accept and walk away knowing
where the gold is hidden.
Play your tricks, pinch my hat if you like
but I will walk away with your golden belt!

Tempted for so long to have a vision of you
I myself have turned into a vision.
You have seized the fortress of my heart,
your love arrows can split even a mountain,
how can my poor heart ever escape them?
I don't even dare to mention your name
and call you "My Moon"
jealous that others may discover you.

This poem is for the time when you held
the cup before me saying,
"Drink, drink now because if you don't,
I will pass the wine to someone else."

You are searching the world for treasure
but the real treasure is yourself.
If you are tempted by bread
you will find only bread.
What you seek for
you become.

I will never leave this house of light, I will never
leave this blessed town
for here I have found my love and here I will stay
for the rest of my life.
If this world turns into a sea of trouble
I will brave the waves and steer my mind's ship
to the safe shore of love.

If you are a seeker looking for profit, go on
and may God be with you,
but I am not willing to exchange my truth,
I have found the heart and will never leave
this house of light.

Get up and whirl around the perfect Master,
why are you clinging to this earth
like a wet flower?
The blessing is in the action.

I wonder
from these thousands of "me's",
which one am I?
Listen to my cry, do not drown my voice
I am completely filled with the thought of you.
Don't lay broken glass on my path
I will crush it into dust.
I am nothing, just a mirror in the palm of your hand,
reflecting your kindness, your sadness, your anger.
If you were a blade of grass or a tiny flower
I would pitch my tent in your shadow.
Only your presence revives my withered heart.
You are the candle that lights the whole world
and I am an empty vessel for your light.

Like a thief
reason sneaked in and sat amongst the lovers
eager to give them advice.
They were unwilling to listen, so reason kissed their feet
and went on its way.

When you see the face of anger
look behind it
and you will see the face of pride.
Bring anger and pride
under your feet, turn them into a ladder
and climb higher.
There is no peace until you become
their master.
Let go of anger, it may taste sweet
but it kills.
Don't become its victim
you need humility to climb to freedom.

My God, do not give me back to myself
do not let me settle for anything but You.
In You I hide escaping from my ruin
please, do not give me back to myself.

Never lose hope
if the Beloved pushes you away,
if He shuts the door on you, don't go,
be patient and wait!
It is your patience that will
draw Him back.
If He blocks all your roads,
be sure
He will show you a secret way
unknown to others.

When at first
love captured my heart
my cries kept the neighbours awake all night.
Now that my love has grown deeper
my cries have calmed down.
When fire catches, smoke
disappears.

I want to be one with you, my love
I am like a madman, tie me with
the curls of your hair.
But if I do not give myself completely,
then complain!

You have withdrawn with the Holy book in your hands,
come and read the book I hold inside my heart,
learn to walk with those who know the way.

You are the musician of the heart,
fill me with your divine music.
You are radiant like Venus, brighter than the moon
charge me with your glance so my eyes
can shine with your love.

Can't you see that your soul is like that of Moses
do not remain a simple shepherd,
leave the flock behind and walk barefoot
on the sacred ground to Mount Sinai.
Your cane can not support you on this path,
you can only lean on Truth.

Your earthly lover
can be very charming and coquettish
but never very faithful.
The true lover is the one who on your final day
opens a thousand doors.

What a loss, what a loss,
to be sober in the midst of drunks.
Keep on pouring the wine of love until
all reason dissolves.
Have you ever seen a thirsty man refuse water?
Fall madly in love, my friend, for reason
is icy cold in the circle of lovers.
Lost in the fog of impressions
reason cannot see the signs of the invisible One.
Finding faults is for those with tired minds.

If you are enslaved by this world remember Joseph,
who never forgot who he was,
become homeless like Jesus, who had no need
for an earthly abode.
If you want to become a seer, do not be
blinded by fear.
You may lose all your veils, so be it!
Be joyous and celebrate!

Joseph has come, the handsome one,
the Jesus of the age has come.
The banner of victory has come
fluttering over the spring parade.
You, whose work is to bring the dead to life,
arise, for that day has come.
The lion, that hunts the lions,
has come to the meadow raging drunk.
Yesterday and the day before are gone,
seize the moment, the time has come.
Today this city is full of excitement,
the Prince has come.
Beat the drum and rejoice for the Friend has come.
A Moon has risen out of the unseen,
compared with which this one is dust.
Because of that Beauty,
the whole world has become restless.
Spread open the skirt of love,
the grace from heaven has come.
You were an exiled bird with cut wings,
rejoice now for your new wings have come.

My imprisoned heart, open your cage,
the one you've lost has come.
Feet dance, for the illustrious King is here.
Speak not of the old man, he is young again,
speak not of yesterday, the Friend has come.
You saw fire and light has come,
you saw blood and red wine has come.
You ran from your good fortune,
now you have come back full of remorse.
Be silent, and count your blessings,
boundless Grace has come.

I said what about my eyes?
"Keep them on the road."
I said what about my passion?
"Keep it burning."
I said what about my heart?
"Tell me what you hold inside it?"
I said pain and sorrow.
He said:
"stay with it."

Telling

the Secret

If you want everlasting glory
don't go back to sleep.
If you want to burn with love
don't go back to sleep.
You have wasted so many nights!
Tonight, for the love of God,
meet the dawn
don't go back to sleep!

You whispered in my ears like early spring:
"I am the call of Love,
can you hear me in the full grasses,
in the scented winds,
it is I who makes the garden smile."

My pure source of life, helper of lovers in despair,
where have you been so long?
Your breathtaking beauty creates such excitement,
such a stir everywhere
that you leave me bewildered.
From the spring of love you bring back
life to my ailing heart.
The song of the awakened earth, the seasons,
the changing Moons,
all this fuss you make is glorious.
Creation bows at your feet.

There is a thread from the heart to the lips
where the secret of life is woven.
Words tear the thread
but in silence
the secrets
speak.

Shall I tell you our secret?
We are charming thieves who steal hearts
and never fail because we are
the friends of the One.
The time for old preaching is over
we aim straight at the heart.
If the mind tries to sneak in and take over
we will string it up without delay.
We turn poison into medicine
and our sorrows into blessings.
All that was familiar,
our loved ones and ourselves
we had to leave behind.

Blessed is the poem that comes through me
but not of me because the sound of my own music
will drown the song of Love.

I was going to tell you my story
but waves of pain drowned my voice.
I tried to utter a word but my thoughts
became fragile and shattered like glass.
Even the largest ship can capsize
in the stormy sea of love,
let alone my feeble boat
which shattered to pieces leaving me nothing
but a strip of wood to hold on to.
Small and helpless, rising to heaven
on one wave of love and falling with the next
I don't even know if I am or I am not.
When I think I am, I find myself worthless,
when I think I am not, I find my value.
Like my thoughts, I die and rise again each day
so how can I doubt the resurrection?
Tired of hunting for love in this world,
at last I surrender in the valley of love
and become free.

I am not a poet
I don't earn my living from poetry.
I don't need to boast of my knowledge.
Poetry is the wine of love
that I accept only from the hands
of my Beloved.

You may be tired and weary
but stay with the lovers
don't run away.
You will either fall in love like me
and if you do not,
just sit and watch.

My master, if you fall asleep
I won't let anyone wake you.
While you sleep your love spreads like a tree
and the fruit sweetens on its branches.

My heart, sit only with those
who know and understand you.
Sit only under a tree
that is full of blossoms.
In the bazaar of herbs and potions
don't wander aimlessly
find the shop with a potion that is sweet.
If you don't have a measure
people will rob you in no time.
You will take counterfeit coins
thinking they are real.
Don't fill your bowl with food from
every boiling pot you see.
Not every joke is humorous, so don't search
for meaning where there isn't one.
Not every eye can see,
not every sea is full of pearls.
My heart, sing the song of longing
like a nightingale.
The sound of your voice casts a spell
on every stone, on every thorn.

First, lay down your head
then one by one
let go of all distractions.
Embrace the light and let it guide you
beyond the winds of desire.
There you will find a spring and
nourished by its sweet waters
like a tree you will bear fruit forever.

When Love comes suddenly and taps
on your window, run and let it in but first,
shut the door of your reason.
Even the smallest hint chases love away
like smoke that drowns the freshness
of the morning breeze.
To reason Love can only say,
the way is barred, you can't pass through
but to the lover it offers a hundred blessings.
Before the mind decides to take a step
Love has reached the seventh heaven.
Before the mind can figure *how*
Love has climbed the Holy Mountain.
I must stop this talk now and let
Love speak from its nest of silence.

If you want to do real work
give your whole heart to it.
Nothing happens just by talking.
A drop of water inside the house
is better than a gushing river outside.

Behind the blood-stained curtains of Love
there are fields of flowers
where the lovers wander.
While the mind sees only boundaries
Love knows the secret way there.
While the mind smells profit and quickly sets up shop
Love sees untold of treasures far beyond.
Lovers trust in the wealth of their hearts
while the all-knowing mind sees only thorns ahead.

To wander in the fields of flowers
pull the thorns from your heart.

Beyond this world and life we know
there is Someone watching over us.
To know Him is not in our power.
But once in a glimpse I saw
that we are His shadow
and our shadow is
the world.

Do not worry if our harp breaks
thousands more will appear.
We have fallen in the arms of love where all is music.
If all the harps in the world were burned down,
still inside the heart
there will be hidden music playing.
Do not worry if all the candles in the world flicker and die
we have the spark that starts the fire.
The songs we sing
are like foam on the surface of the sea of being
while the precious gems lie deep beneath.
But the tenderness in our songs
is a reflection of what is hidden in the depths.
Stop the flow of your words,
open the window of your heart and
let the spirit speak.

Hidden from all
I will speak to you without words.
No one but you will hear my story
even if I tell it in the middle of the crowd.

The secrets are bursting inside me
but to give them away and
expose them to mockery, I cannot.
Something inside me is bursting with joy
but to put my finger on it, I cannot.

When you plant a tree
every leaf that grows will tell you,
what you sow will bear fruit.
So if you have any sense, my friend
don't plant anything but love,
you show your worth by what you seek.
Water flows to those who want purity
wash your hands of all desires and
come to the table of Love.

Do you want me to tell you a secret?
The flowers attract the most beautiful lover
with their sweet smile and scent.
If you let God weave the verse in your poem
people will read it forever.

There comes a time
when sea and land come to rest.
There comes a time
when even the heavens withdraw.
There comes a time
when weary travellers
need a rest from the journey.

Let us fall in love again
and scatter gold dust all over the world.
Let us become a new spring
and feel the breeze drift in the heavens' scent.
Let us dress the earth in green,
and like the sap of a young tree
let the grace from within sustain us.
Let us carve gems out of our stony hearts
and let them light our path to Love.
The glance of Love is crystal clear
and we are blessed by its light.

The
Cure is
in the Pain

Beloved, you are my salvation
my only companion, my retreat and guide,
but you are also the one who breaks my heart.
You are my Noah, my soul
the conquered and the conqueror.
Open my heart and sweep it clean
from all my secrets.
You are Grace enveloped in light,
kindness and wrath,
a drop and the vast ocean
how long will you torment me?
My Sun, my flicker of hope,
do not let me die of thirst
for you are the water and the cup
you are my pain and my cure.
Release me from the web of the body
and keep my heart by your side.

Our Judge is not like any other
His judgement is never cruel.
From the dawn of time
He has been in love with Love
and only Love will satisfy Him.

I have come to drag you out of your self
and take you in my heart.
I have come to bring out the beauty
you never knew you had
and lift you like a prayer to the sky.
If no one can recognize you, I do
because you are my life and soul.
Don't run away, accept your wounds and
let bravery be your shield.
It takes a thousand stages
for the perfect being to evolve.
Every step of the way I will walk with you
and never leave you stranded.
Be patient, do not open the lid too soon
simmer away until you are ready.
In this game I make the rules.
I roll you like a ball and chase you
when I choose.

In a dream my lover came
searching through my body
for the state of love.
When he could not find it
he drew his dagger and stabbed
my heart.

Don't take the cup away from me
before I've had enough to drink.
Your promises are charming
but I am not a fool.
Be more giving or I will have to rob you,
you raise your price to discourage me
but I am not naive and won't give up so easily.
Come out of hiding, open the door and let me in
I am at your mercy, the slave of your smile.
I put on airs to impress you,
even your scolding inflames my passion.
You are the music within music that stole my heart.
If I see beauty it's because I look through your eyes
but when I come back to myself
I find no one there.
Still you are not content, what more do you want?
My king, I am your falcon and when I hear your drum
I will spread my wings.
If you offer me your love I'll be drunk with joy,
but if you do not, I will accept,
lower my head and surrender.

I am ill with fever
His fiery words burned my heart.
No medicine can help me
other than the wine and sweet nectar
from the lips of my Beloved.

We are healers, wise men from the East!
We have cured many from sorrow and blindness,
we uproot the cause of all pain.
We bring the dead to life because
we have learned our skills from Christ,
ask those who have witnessed our signs.
We mix our medicine from plants of paradise
and need no instruments
for we run through the body like thought.
We are the healers of spirit and
do not look for reward.

But before we leave,
remember not to speak of us, guard your words
for this world is full of unfriendly ears.

I am in love not only
with his smile and radiant face
but also with his wrath and contempt.
He has asked for my head
I do not care if I lose it
what makes me ecstatic is
Him asking.

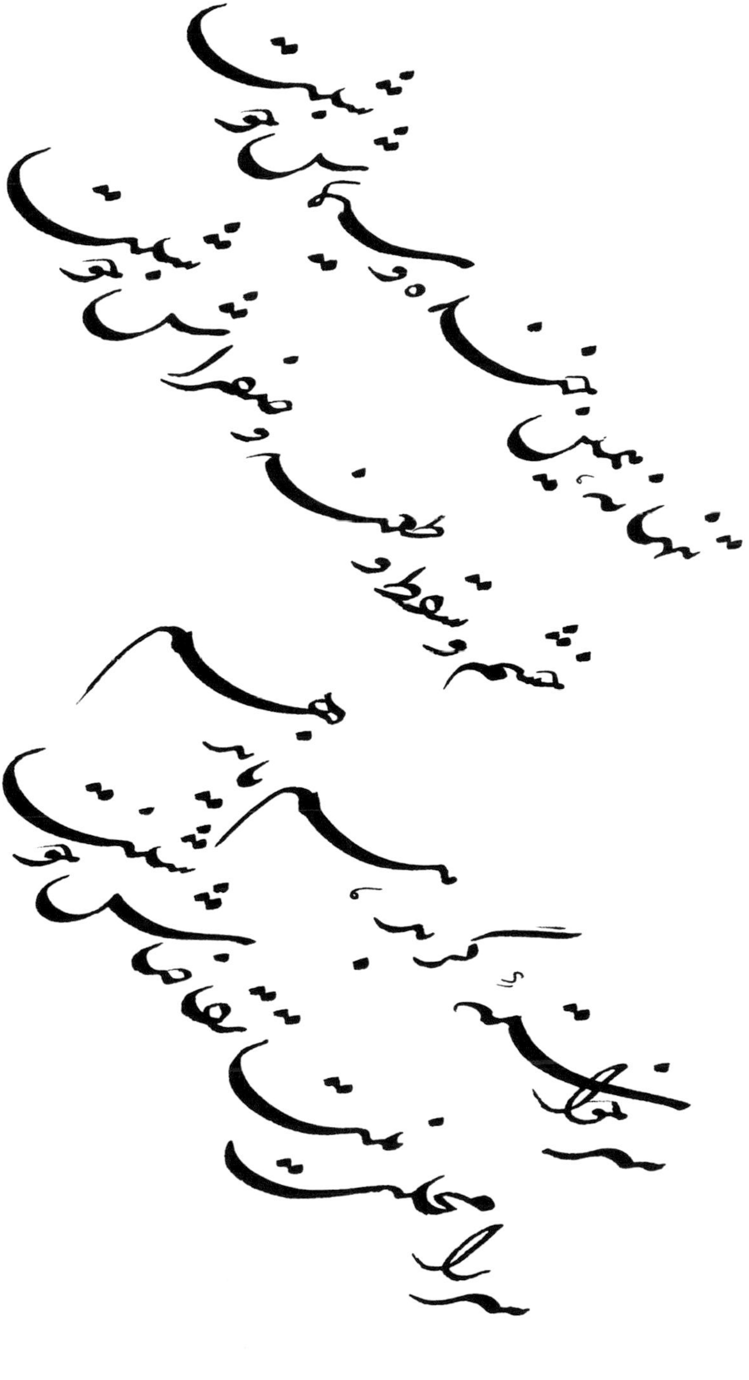

The Friend has rejected me
He has broken my heart and shut the door.
Now my desolate heart and I
will sit patiently on his doorstep
for He loves those with a broken heart.

Why are you so afraid of silence,
silence is the root of everything.
If you spiral into its void
a hundred voices will thunder messages
you long to hear.

You came suddenly like resurrection,
like an infinite blessing
and my thoughts burned like trees on fire.
You came today like God Himself,
generous and full of grace,
holding the key to my freedom in your hands.
Both traveller and the road,
the beginning and the end,
You are the gatekeeper of the Sun.
For so long I have lived in pain, suspended
between my longing and my need for bread.
Now that You have risen in my heart
and taken over my thoughts,
I am breaking the pen and leaving the paper.

My Sun has risen!

If you befriend the Beloved
you will never be lonely.
If you learn to be flexible
you will never be helpless.
The moon shines because it
does not escape the night.
The rose is scented because it
has embraced the thorn.

My body pulled my soul from the higher planes
and I lost the company of saints and prophets.
Now wrapped in my prison I've met a Moon
that fills my heart with dreams and visions.
Most people want to escape from prison
but why should I run away when my love is inside,
where else could I be alone with love?
I look at myself and see such painful longing
I look at love and see how pleased she is watching me.
Once you are in that house of Beauty
abundant grace awaits you.

I overheard the stars whispering
that if ever one of them
caught a glimpse of that Beauty,
to tell the others at once.
But the lovers guard their secrets jealously
for they know that when that Moon rises
everything will set.

One day your heart
will take you to your lover.
One day your soul
will carry you to the Beloved.
Don't get lost in your pain,
know that one day
your pain will become your cure.

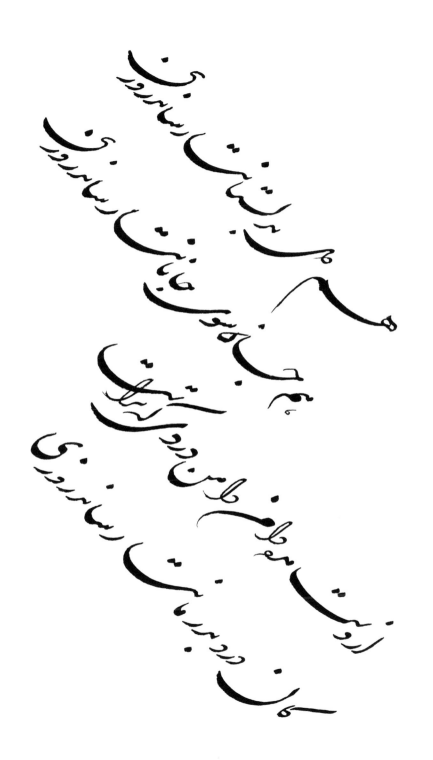

You are the sky and I am the earth
astonished at what you grow inside my heart.
Dry-lipped and thirsty, only the grace of your rain
can turn the earth into a rose garden.
By you it is pregnant and only you know its burden.
It twists, it turns and sighs until
it gives birth to divine longing.

The Beloved takes care of his lovers
and feeds them generously.
Sometimes he ties them with the cord of reason
and sometimes he sets them free to dance.
Look at the meadow bursting with flowers
unable to contain its joy.
Look at the power of the Divine One
turning senseless dust into a sublime painting!
All we see is a veil of this never setting Sun,
this ancient Sun that will one day silently reveal
everything that has been planted.

When something unique becomes many,
it loses its value.
Yet many are the sorrows of the heart
but they become precious gems
on the path to the Beloved.

My tired heart, take a sigh of relief
the time has come for you to heal.
The friend who helps all lovers
has come into this world
in the form of
a man.

Never linger too long with the ignorant,
throw stones at their talk.
Walk only with the lovers,
the mirror of the soul gets rusty when
dipped in muddy water.

I am drunk and you are insane
tell me, who will lead us home?
How many times have I asked you not to drink so much
for I see no sober soul in town.
Come to the tavern my dearest and taste the wine of love
for the soul is joyous only in the company of lovers.
The tavern of love is your livelihood
your income and expenses, the wine.
Be careful, not to trust a sober soul
with even one drop of this wine.
Go on playing your lute, my drunken gypsy but tell me,
between the two of us, who is more drunk?
As I left my house a Sufi approached me,
in his glance I saw a hundred gardens.
He swayed from side to side like a ship without an anchor,
while a hundred reasonable men watched on enviously.
Where are you from? I asked him.
He replied, "Half from Turkistan and half from Farghaneh,
half from water and clay and half from soul and heart,
half from the edge of the sea and half from the depths
of the ocean."

Then I am no stranger to you, I said and asked him
to befriend me.
He said, "I make no distinctions between friends and strangers.
I've lost my heart and thrown away my turban
to dwell in the tavern of love.
My heart is heavy with words I want to say to you.
I have given you this advice before but you ignored it.
If you live with the lame you will only learn to limp."
Once the Prophet leaned against a tree to rest
and when he left even the tree cried from the pain of separation.
Shams, now that you have stirred my heart do not desert me!

Last night I gave a star a message for you.
On my knees I begged her to tell you
how much I pray that you turn my stony heart
golden with your radiance.
I bared my chest to show my wounds and
asked her to tell you that if I sway this way and that
it's because I need to calm the infant of my heart,
for babies sleep when rocked in their cradle.
My Beloved, my heart was yours always
nurse it like a child, save it from wandering.
How long will you keep me in exile?
I will be quiet now but even in my silence
my heart will long for the glance of your grace.

Look at me, I am your Friend
on the night when you leave the house of your body
I will be with you in the grave.
You will hear my voice and know that
we were never separated.
I am the lucid core of your being
I've been by your side in joy and suffering.
On that fateful night you will hear my familiar voice,
see the lit candles and smell the sweet incense.
I will bring you food and wine.
On that night you will hear the blast of the trumpet
that will rip open the shrouds of the dead.
On that night the dust of all ages will be stirred
by the glory of the resurrection.
Don't look for me in human shape for
the soul is subtle and love is jealous.
There is no place for form in love.

Someone is
Hidden Inside

Here someone is hidden
who has taken hold of me and does not let me go.

Here someone is hidden
softer than the soul who led me to the garden of spirit
and made me homeless.

Here someone is hidden
a radiant face as delicate and fleeting
as the ephemeral moment before sleep.

Here someone is hidden
like sweetness in sugar cane,
an invisible magician who has captured my soul.

Hidden somewhere inside, my beloved and I
have dissolved in each other.

No beauty in the world can ever tempt me
for I see only the face of my Beloved.
Tired and in pain I searched the world for help
until I found in love the cure for my pain.

Here someone hidden whispered:
"Pass beyond your tears and
you will see the broken hearted lovers
are the lords in heaven."

Here someone hidden appeared
holding love's wine
and to him I've given all my vows.

Pilgrims
why are you turning round in circles,
what are you looking for?
The Beloved is here, why search in the desert?
If you look deep in your heart
you will find Him within yourself.
You have made the pilgrimage and
trod the path to Mecca many times.
You rave about the holy place
and say you've visited God's garden
but where is your bunch of flowers?
You tell stories about diving deep into the ocean
but where is your pearl?
There is some merit
in the suffering you have endured
but what a pity you have not discovered
the Mecca that's inside.

It is not the lover's fault
that he is so refined.
It is not the lover's fault that
he is so beautiful and delicate.
His only fault is that
he has no fault.

If you bake bread with the wheat that grows on my grave
you'll become drunk with joy and
even the oven will recite ecstatic poems.
If you come to pay your respects
even my gravestone will invite you to dance
so don't come without your drum.
Don't be sad. You have come to God's feast.
Even death cannot stop my yearning
for the sweet kiss of my love.
Tear my shroud and wear it as a shirt,
the door will open and you'll hear
the music of your soul fill the air.
I am created from the ecstasy of love and
when I die, my essence will be released
like the scent of crushed rose petals.
My soul wants to leap and join
the towering soul of Shams.

It seems a lifetime since
I have seen your enchanted garden.
You hide from the crowds invisible like devotion.
Oh, it has been so long since
I have seen your face.

My heart, make friends with grief
and if you do, what luck!
Embrace it for your grief is the call
the Beloved answers.

I can't pretend to be a lion able to conquer the enemy
to master myself would be enough.
I am only the dust on my Lover's path and from dust
I will rise and turn into a flower.
Dark like the night I mourn and hold the pain
of love inside me.
But bright like the Moon I will rise from the darkness
for I have seen the source of light and being a child
whose tutor is love I will not grow up ignorant.
I will rise like a flame out of love's fire
and become infinite like love.
When I reach my end, play the music
that will lift me up to Spirit.

You have woken up late,
lost and perplexed
but don't rush to your books
looking for knowledge.
Pick up the flute instead and
let your heart play.

Who is in the house of my heart,
I cried in the middle of the night.
Love said,
"It is I, but what are all these images that fill your house?"
I said, they are the reflection of your beautiful face.
She asked,
"But what is this image full of pain?"
I said, it is me lost in the sorrows of life
and showed her my soul full of wounds.
She offered me one end of a thread and said:
"Take it so I can pull you back
but do not break the delicate string."
I reached towards her but she struck my hand.
I asked, why the harshness?
She said,
"To remind you that whoever comes to love's holy space,
proud and full of himself will be sent away.
Look at love with the eyes of your heart."

Your generosity is vaster than the sea
it does not wait for tomorrow.
No need to ask You for anything.
Does anyone ever ask the Sun for light?

Didn't I tell you
do not leave me for I am your only Friend,
I am the spring of life.
Even if you leave in anger for thousands of years
you will come back to me for I am your goal and your end.
Didn't I tell you
not to be seduced by this colorful world
for I am the Ultimate Painter.
Didn't I tell you
you are a fish do not go to dry land
for I am the deep Sea.
Didn't I tell you
not to fall in the net like birds
for I am your wings and the power of flight.
Didn't I tell you
not to let them change your mind and turn you to ice
for I am your fire and warmth.

Didn't I tell you
they will corrupt you and make you forget
that I am the Spring of all virtues.
Didn't I tell you
not to question my actions
for everything falls into order, I am the Creator.
Didn't I tell you
your heart can guide you home
because it knows that I am your Master.

The spring is smiling, the table is set in the garden
the wine is poured and the candle is lit,
but if you are not there, my love
what is the use of it all?
And where you are
what else do I
need?

I only speak of the Sun
because the Sun is my Master
I worship even the dust at His feet.
I am not a night-lover and do not praise sleep
I am the messenger of the Sun!
Secretly I will ask Him and pass the answers to you.
Like the Sun I shine on those who are forsaken
I may look drunk and dishevelled but I speak the Truth.
Tear off the mask, your face is glorious,
your heart may be cold as stone but
I will warm it with my raging fire.
No longer will I speak of sunsets or rising Moons,
I will bring you love's wine
for I am born of the Sun
I am a King!

What a blessing, my lover came to me.
I asked the night to keep our secret.
But can't you see, said the night,
you are holding the Sun
how can I bring
the dawn?

If you are eager to be nothing
before you know who you are,
you rob yourself of your true being.
Until you understand *nothingness*
you will never know true Faith.

Hidden from all eyes and ears
let us tell each other of our soul.
Smile like a rose with no lips
and keep silent like a thought.
Let us speak silently the secret like Spirit
and avoid talkers who use words in vain.
Let us join our hands
listen to every flutter of our heart
let us become one in silence.
Divine destiny knows our fate to the last detail
let our story be told in a silent way.

In my ear love murmurs
my soul has fainted.
All colors melt in
Love's transparent sky
I am only an empty cup.

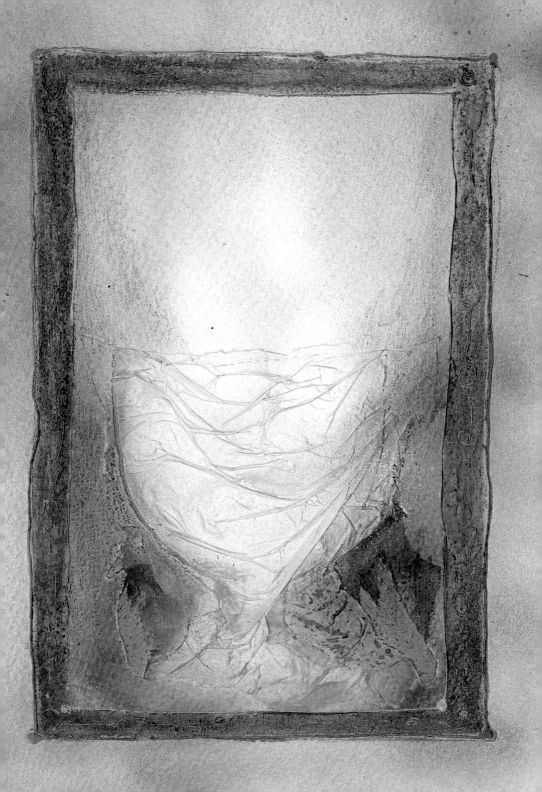

Tonight is the essence of all nights
when you can ask for your deepest wish.
Tonight is the night of the one
who shares God's secrets.

Please God, offer honey to musicians
who bring us such joy!
Give them strong and untiring hands
to keep playing their music.
Give them vision so, like birds in love,
they can bring Your message to our ears.
Let them drink plenty from Your river and
grace them with Your strength
so their music becomes the pillar of Your glory.

Where is that Moon
that never rises or sets?
Where is that soul
that is neither with nor without us?
Don't say it is here or there.
All creation is Him but
for the eyes that can see.

One day
You will take my heart completely
and make it more fiery than
a dragon.
Your eyelashes will write on my heart
the poem
that could never come from the pen
of a poet.

Let us Begin the Journey

Wake up lovers, it is time to start the journey!
We have seen enough of this world, it is time to see another.

These two gardens may be beautiful but
let us pass beyond them and go to the Gardener.

Let us kiss the ground and flow like a river
towards the ocean.

Let us go from the valley of tears to the wedding feast,
let us bring the color of blossoms to our pale faces.

Our hearts shiver like autumn leaves about to fall,
in this world of dust there is no avoiding pain or feeling exiled.

Let us become like beautifully colored birds
and fly to the sweet land of paradise.

Everything is painted with the brush of the Invisible One
let us follow the hidden signs and find the Painter.

It is best to travel with companions
on this perilous journey only love can lead the way.

We are like rain splashing on a roof
let us find our way down the spout.

We are like an arched bow with the arrow in place
let us become straight and release the arrow towards the target.

We have stayed at home scared like mice
let us find our courage and join the lions.

Let our souls turn into a mirror
longing to reflect the essence of Beauty.

Let us begin the journey home.

To find a pearl dive deep into the ocean
don't look in fountains.
To find a pearl you must
emerge from the water of life always thirsty.

Wake up in the morning breeze
to the call for prayer and hear
the music fill the air.
Rejoice
and fill your cup with the wine of love.
Pass it around, pass it to me first,
so I can be drunk with ecstasy
but bind my feet so I don't wander.
My life, my strength, my faith are in your hands.
Launch me in the sea of love
and let me sail.

Shams, you are the Lord of all Kings
your words are my eternal treasure.

Do you hear what the music is saying?
"Come follow me and you will find the way.
Your mistakes can also lead you to the truth.
When you ask, the answer will be given."

A baby pigeon on the edge of the nest
hears the call and begins his flight.
How can the soul of the seeker not fly
when a message arrives saying,
"You have been trapped in life like a bird
with no wings,
in a cage with no doors or windows
come, come back to me!"
How can the soul not rip open its coverings,
and soar to the sky.
What is the rope that pulls the soul from above?
What is the secret that opens the door?
The key is the flutter of the heart's wings
and its endless longing.
When the door opens, walk on the path
where abundance awaits you,
where everything old becomes new
and never look back.
Drink from the hands of the wine bearer
and you will be blessed
even in this life.

If you can't smell the fragrance
don't come into the garden of Love.
If you are unwilling to undress
don't enter into the stream of Truth.
Stay where you are, don't come our way.

I am that black night who hates the Moon.
I am that wretched beggar who is
angry with the King.
Out of kindness He calls me in but I am angry
and invent excuses.
I have lost my peace but I will not sigh,
I am angry at sighing!
I had my chances for wealth and power
now I don't want them
I am angry.
I flee from the Magnet, I am a straw resisting
the pull of the Amber.
We are only tiny particles helpless in this world
I am angry with God!
You don't know how it feels to drown
you are out of the sea of love.
You are only a shadow of the Sun and
I am angry with the shadows!

Do not be flattered by reason,
reason is only
the child of the mind.
But true friendship
is born out of love and
is the water of life.
The footprints of the Friend
are all over the world
follow them and walk into life.

I can be without anyone
but not without you.
You twist my heart, dwell in my mind
and fill my eyes, you are my joy
I can't be without you.
You are my sleep, my rest, the water I drink.
You are my clarity, my dignity, my world
I can't be without you.
Sometimes you are kind, sometimes unfaithful,
you break my heart but
my love, my essence, do not go away
I can't be without you.
You are the head I am the feet
you are the hand, I am your banner
if you leave, I will perish
I can't be without you.
You have erased my image, taken my sleep
you've torn me away from everybody but
I can't be without you.
I find no joy in life or relief in death.
Why don't you say it too
I can't be without you.

My heart, do not take pride in
every thought,
do not flutter like a moth around
every light.
Until you know yourself
you will be distant from
God.

I am the Spirit Moon
with no place.
You do not see me for I am hidden
inside the soul.
Others want you for themselves but I call you
back to yourself.
You give me many names but I am
beyond all names.
Sometimes you say I am deceitful
but as long as you are
I will be too.
Until you remain blind and deaf
I will be invisible.
I am the garden of all gardens
I speak as the King of all flowers
I am the spring of all waters.
My words are like a ship and the sea
is their meaning.
Come to me and I will take you
to the depths of spirit.

From the heart of the lovers, blood flows
like a vast river.
Our body is the windmill and love,
the water.
Without water the mill cannot turn.

I've had enough
no more patience left.
I will give away your secret.
My heart is burning in this blazing fire,
drunk with pain.
I've had enough
I will give away your ancient secret.
You can choose to listen or not.

Lost in the grip of my passion,
I heard the Moon saying,
"Am I not your friend and companion
why do you want to betray me?"

Startled, I looked at that Beauty,
at my life giver, my soul's music,
the water for my burning heart
and promised
to keep her secret forever.

Awakened by your love
I flicker like a candle
trying to hold on in the dark.
Yet, you spare me no blows and
keep asking,
'Why do you complain?'

What was in that bright candlelight
that took my heart and burned it so completely?

Come back, my friend, come quickly
nothing can heal me but your sweetness.

I remember a dawn when my heart
untied a lock of your hair.

My soul heard something from your soul
my heart drank from your spring.

I drowned and the flood swept me away.

Do not look back, my friend
no one knows how the world ever began.
Do not fear the future, nothing lasts forever.
If you dwell on the past or the future
you will miss the moment.

When I see your face
I shut my eyes to others.
I am drunk with your presence.
To earn Solomon's seal
I have become supple as wax.
When I see your face
I surrender my will and
become a sigh on your lips.
You were in my hand but I kept reaching out
like a blind man.
I was in your hand but kept asking questions
from those who are ignorant.
I must have been very drunk or naive
to steal my own gold,
I must have been mad to sneak in
and rob my own jasmine garden.
I've been twisted long enough by your might,
Shams of Tabriz!
But even in my sorrow I am joyous
like the crescent moon
at the beginning of the festival.

My dear heart
never think you are better than others.
Listen to their sorrows with compassion.
If you want peace, don't harbor bad thoughts
do not gossip and
don't teach what you do not know.

Die, die inside this love
and rise in Spirit.
Die, die and cut the ego's rope
that holds you a prisoner.
Take an axe to the wall and
dig a way out of the prison.
Die, die before the beautiful King
you will become mighty.
Die, die and rise out of this cloud
you will shine like the glorious moon.
Be silent, be silent,
for silence is the sure sign of death.
From your silence
life will trumpet louder than sound.

Whoever plants the seed of devotion
takes that seed from the divine harvest.
Whoever plays music with joy
is moved by divine inspiration
but doesn't know it.

You have fallen in love my dear heart
Congratulations!

You have freed yourself from all attachments
Congratulations!

You have given up both worlds to be on your own
the whole creation praises your solitude
Congratulations!

Your disbelief has turned into belief
your bitterness, into sweetness
Congratulations!

You have now entered into Love's fire, my pure heart
Congratulations!

Inside the Sufi's heart there is always a feast
dear heart, you are celebrating
Congratulations!

My heart, I have seen how your tears turned into a sea
now every wave keeps saying
Congratulations!

O silent lover, seeker of the higher planes,
may the Beloved always be with you
Congratulations!

You have struggled hard, may you grow wings and fly
Congratulations!

Keep silent my dear heart, you have done so well
Congratulations!

Terms and Symbolism

Beloved, Friend, King	God in His loving aspect
The lover	The *Sufi* in search of the Beloved
Burning	The process of purification of the soul
Darvish, Dervish	*Sufi* mystic
Drunk, drunkenness	Intoxication with the love of God
Reed	Longing for return to the source
Killing	Breaking one's attachment to the ego
Nightingale	Symbol of the soul's longing
Ocean	The limitless universe of God
Rose	Symbol of the beauty of the Beloved
Rose-garden	Paradise and eternal beauty
Sema, Sama	Spiritual whirling dance of the *darvishes*
Sufi	Mystic in search of the Beloved
Wine	Symbol of the ecstasy of the love of God
Veil	Symbolizes the layers of the ego that separate the Self from the Beloved
Joseph	The son of Jacob, symbol of Divine Beauty

Sources

Badiozaman Forouzanfar, *Divan Shams*, Tehran, Iran, Amir Kabir Publishers, 1336/1957

Mohamad Reza Shafii Kadkani, *Selections of Divan*, Tehran, Iran, Amir Kabir Publishers, 1375/1996

Index

D – Divan of Shams
R – Rubai
SK – Selection of Divan by Shafii Kadkani

Sun and Moon

The Path

Plant the Seed of Truth

Telling the Secret

The Cure is in the Pain

Someone is Hidden Inside

Let us Beging the Journey